Muse & Drudge

Muse & Drudge

Harryette Mullen
Singing Horse

Acknowledgements

  I praise my publisher, Gil Ott, for his commitment, vision, and empathy as I wrote and revised this manuscript. I am grateful to the editors of the following publications, where parts of *Muse & Drudge* have previously appeared: *Agni Review, Antioch Review, Arras, The Best American Poetry 1994, Bombay Gin, Callaloo, Chain, hole, Long News in the Short Century, lower limit speech, Muleteeth, On the Verge, Proliferation, Prosodia, VLS (Village Voice Literary Supplement).*

  I have also had the pleasure of a long-distance collaboration with T.J. Anderson, who set portions of *Muse & Drudge* to music in his *Seven Cabaret Songs*, composed in Bellagio, Italy on a commission from the Mallarme Chamber Players, with support from the North Carolina Arts Council. The world premiere of this work, scheduled for fall 1995, will feature jazz vocalist Nnenna Freelon and the Mallarme Chamber Players.

Cover photograph by Harvey Finkle.
Cover design by Harryette Mullen and Judith Natal.
Typesetting by Friends Journal.

ISBN 0-935162-15-1

Published by: SINGING HORSE PRESS
          PO Box 40034
          Philadelphia PA 19106
          (215)844-7678

Fatten your animal for sacrifice, poet,
but keep your muse slender.

—Callimachus

Sapphire's lyre styles
plucked eyebrows
bow lips and legs
whose lives are lonely too

my last nerve's lucid music
sure chewed up the juicy fruit
you must don't like my peaches
there's some left on the tree

you've had my thrills
a reefer a tub of gin
don't mess with me I'm evil
I'm in your sin

clipped bird eclipsed moon
soon no memory of you
no drive or desire survives
you flutter invisible still

another funky Sunday
stone-souled picnic
your heart beats me
as I lie naked on the grass

a name determined by other names
prescribed mediation
unblushingly on display
to one man or all

traveling Jane
no time to settle down
bee in her bonnet
her ants underpants

bittersweet and inescapable
hip signals like later
some handsome man kind on the eyes
a kind man looks good to me

I dream a world
and then what
my soul is resting
but my feet are tired

half the night gone
I'm holding my own
some half forgotten tune
casual funk from a darker back room

handful of gimme
myself when I am real
how would you know
if you've never tasted

a ramble in brambles
the blacker more sweeter juicier
pores sweat into blackberry tangles
going back native natural country wild briers

country clothes hung on her all and sundry
bolt of blue have mercy ink perfume
that snapping turtle pussy
won't let go until thunder comes

call me pessimistic
but I fall for sour pickles
sweets for the heat
awrr reet peteet patootie

shadows crossed her face
distanced by the medium
riffing through it
too poor to pay attention

sepia bronze mahogany
say froggy jump salty
jelly in a vise
buttered up broke ice

sun goes on shining
while the debbil beats his wife
blues played lefthanded
topsy-turvy inside out

under the weather
down by the sea
a broke johnny walker
mister meaner

bigger than a big man
cirrus as a heart attracts
more power than a loco motive
think your shit don't stink

edge against a wall
wearing your colors
soulfully worn out
stylishly distressed

battered like her face
embrazened with ravage
the oxidizing of these
agonizingly worked surfaces

that other scene offstage
where by and for her he descends
a path through tangled sounds
he wants to make a song

blue gum pine barrens
loose booty muddy bosom
my all day contemplation
my midnight dream

something must need fixing
raise your window high
the carpenter's here
with hammer and nail

what you do to me
got to tell it
sing it shout out
all about it

ketchup with reality
built for meat wheels
the diva road kills
comfort shaking on the bones

trouble in mind
naps in the back
if you can't stand
sit in your soul kitsch

pot said kettle's mama must've
burnt them turnip greens
kettle deadpanned not missing a beat
least mine ain't no skillet blonde

sue for slender
soften her often
mamiwata weaves
rolexical glitter

get a new mouth
don't care what it costs
smell that hot sauce
shake it down south

the purify brothers
clamor for rhythm
ain't none of they business
till the ring is on the finger

breaks wet thigh high stepper
bodacious butt shakes
rebellious riddem
older than black pepper

deja voodoo queens
rain flooded graves in New Orleans
sex model dysfunction
ruint a guest's vacation

figures with lit wicks
time to make a switch
rumba with the chains removed
folkways of the turf

black dispatch do do run run
through graffiti brierpatch
scratch a goofered grapevine telegraph
drums the wires they hum

mad dog kiwi antifreezes
green spittle anguished folks
downwind skidrowed elbow greasers
monkey wrench nuts and bolts

my skin but not my kin
my race but not my taste
my state and not my fate
my country not my kunk

how a border orders disorder
how the children looked
whose mothers worked
in the maquiladora

where to sleep in stormy weather
Patel hotel with swell hot plate
women's shelter under a sweater
friends don't even recognize my face

tombstone disposition
is to graveyard mind
as buzzard luck
to beer pocketbook

the backwoods deflated whip
blank North America skies
rag dolls made of black scraps
with pearl button eyes

random diva nation of bedlam
headman hoodlum doodling then I
wouldn't be long gone
I'd be Dogon

down there shuffling coal
humble materials hold
vestiges of toil
the original cutting tool

splendid and well-made
presenting no disturbance
the natural order of things
between man and himself

try others but none lasted
a shame they went that way
missing referents murking it up
with clear actors lacking

too tough is tough enough
to walk these dirty streets with us
too loud too strong too black bad
too many desires you've never met

butch knife
cuts cut
opening open
flower flowers flowering

scratched out hieroglyphs
the songs of allusion
and even the motion
changing of our own violins

cough drops prick thick
orange ink remover inside
people eating tuna fish
treat the architecture to pesticides

elaborate trash
disparaged rags
if I had my rage
I'd tear the blueprint up

chained thus together
voice held me hostage
divided our separate ways
with a knife against my throat

black dream you came
sleep chilled stuttering spirit
drunk on apple ripple
still in my dark unmarked grave

ain't cut drylongso
her songs so many-hued
hum some blues in technicolor
pick a violet guitar

emblems of motion
muted amused mulish
there's more to love
where that came from

heavy model chevy of yore
old time religion
low down get real down
get right with Godzilla

write on the vagina
of virgin lamb paper
mother times mirror
divided by daughter

soulless divaism
incog iconicism
a dead straight head
the spectrum wasted

dicty kickpleat
beats deadbeats
hussified dozens
womanish like you groan

belly to belly
iron pot and cauldron
close to home
the core was melting

head maid in made out
house of swank kickback
placage conquer bind
lemon melon melange

if you've been in Virginia
where the green grass grows
did you send your insignia
up a greased flagpole

you used to hock your hambone
at a cock and bull pawnshop
got your start as a sideman
now you're big on your own

what makes tough muffins
pat Juba on the back
Miz Mary takes a mack truck in
trade for her slick black cadillac

la muerte dropped her token
in the subway slot machine
nobody told the green man
the fortune cookie lied

keep your powder dry
your knees together
your dress down
your drawers shut

a picture perfect
twisted her limbs
lovely as a tree
for art's sake

muse of the world picks
out stark melodies
her raspy fabric
tickling the ebonies

you can sing their songs
with words your way
put it over to the people
know what you doing

curly waves away blues navy
saved from salvation
army grits and gravy
tries no lie relaxation

some little bitter
spilled glitter
wiped the floor
with spoiled sugar

back dating double dutch
fresh out of bubble gum
halfstep in the grave
on banana peels of love

devils dancing on a dime
cut a rug in ragtime
jitterbug squat diddly bow
stark strangled banjo

how you feel when it's windy
something blue on you
speak to the feeling
consolate your mind

many strong and soon
these seeds open wings
float down parachutes
then try one more again

copulation from scratch
kisses go down hard
no weekday self
makes it bleed

edges sharpened
remove the blur
enhance the image
of dynamic features

dark-eyed flower
knuckling under
lift a finger for her
give the lady a hand

not her hard life
cramped hot stages
only her approach
ahead of the beat

live in easy virtue
where days behaving send
her dance and her body
forward to a new air dress

a pad for writing
where dreams hit el cielo
crack the plaster fool mood rising
it's snowing on the radio

honey jars of hair
skin and nail conjuration
a racy make-up artist collects herself
in time for a major retrospection

her lady's severe beauty
and downright manner
enhance the harsh landscape
positioned with urban product

mule for hire or worse
beast of burden down when I lay
clean and repair the universe
lawdy lawdy hallelujah when I lay

tragic yellow mattress
belatedly beladied blues
shines staggerly avid diva
ruses of the lunatic muse

odds meeting on a bus
the wrecked cognition
calling baby sister
what sounds like abuse

you have the girl you paid for
now lie on her
rocky garden
I build my church

a world for itself
where music comes to itself
three thirds of heaven
sure to be raining

on her own jive
player and instrument
all the way live
the way a woman might use it

sugar shack full
of fat sweaty ladies
women of size with men
who love too much

what is inward
wanting to get out
prey to the lard
trying to pass for butter

cakewalk matrix
tapping the frets
dubbed and mastered
tucked into the folds

kiss my black bottom
good and plenty
where the doorknob split
the sun don't shine

it's rank it cranks you up
crash you're fracked you suck
shucks you're wack you be
all you cracked up to be

dead on arrival
overdosed on whatever
excess of hate and love
I sleep alone

if you were there
then please come in
tell me what's good
think up something

psychic sidekick
gimme a pigfoot
show me my lifeline
read me my rights

in Dahomey the royal umbrella
roof sky tree dome
heads up the procession of saints
balling the jack back home

framed in her snake-relief decorated doorway
bordered with zigzag deer legs
the notched beam is a stepladder
dried millet a sign of hospitality

this art is fast disappearing
indigenous pigments learned from their mothers
earth from the river
fingers and hands

men harnessed mules
rode hard put away wet
on the brine sea
unwed men toss and sweat

dark rain laden clouds
fragrant womb
from pyramid to palm
the black tide of mud

calabash of water
botanica Yoruba
latecomers to a potboiler
plot rebellion in the quarter

under the drinking gourd
they stood in a word
free despite thirst
lovely in their dust

torn veins stitched
together with pine needles
mended hands fix
the memory of a people

go ahead and sing the blues
then ask for forgiveness
you can't do everything
and still be saved

update old records
tune around the verses
fast time and swing out
head set in a groove

felt some good sounds
but didn't have the time
sing it in my voice
put words in like I want them

noise in the market
my mustang done slowed down
tore up bad now
put a ruination on it

bring money bring love
lucky floorwash seven
powers of Africa la mano
poderosa ayudame numeros sueños

restore lost nature
with hoodoo paraphernalia
get cured in Cuban by a charming
shaman in an urban turban

forgotten formula cures
endemic mnemonic plague
statisticians were sure
the figures were vague

sister mystery listens
helps souls in misery
get to the square root
of evil and render it moot

wine's wicked wine's divine
pickled drunk down to the rind
depression ham ain't got no bone
watermelons rampant emblazoned

island name Dawta
Gullah backwater
she swim she fish
here it be fresh

cassava yucca taro dasheen
spicy yam okra vinegary greens
guava salt cod catfish ackee
fatmeat's greasy that's too easy

not to be outdone she put
the big pot in the little pot
when you get food this good
you know the cook stuck her foot in it

they pass their good air
mixed with fresh fair
complex ions somewhere
frimpted frone she's stand alone

female of the specifically
human woman not called
by dog or dug by some tool -- no fool who
takes stray pets or rakes implements for compliments

what I do with my hats
they make their own parade
of float and glitter like birds
adorn the open umbrella

my dreams could take
advantage of me and no
one would tell me because
they don't know where to reach me

mothers have spawned
what warriors now own
cruel emblems and secrets
divulged only to the adept

signs in the heavens
graphemes leave the trees
turning over fresh pages
of notation: a choreography for bees

cooter got her back scratched
with spirit scribble
sent down under water
with some letters for the ancestors

the folks shuffle off
this mortal coffle and
bamboula back to
the motherland

why these blues come from us
threadbare material soils
the original colored
pregnant with heavenly spirit

stop running from the gift
slow down to catch up with it
knots mend the string quilt
of kente stripped when kin split

white covers of black material
dense fabric that obeys its own logic
shadows pieced together tears and all
unfurling sheets of bluish music

burning cloth in a public place
a crime against the state
raised the cost of free expression
smoke rose to offer a blessing

with all that rope they gave us
we pulled a mule out of the mud
dragging backwoods along
in our strong blackward progress

she just laughs
at weak-kneed scarecrow
as rainbow crow flies
over those ornery cornrows

everlasting arms
too short for boxers
leaning meaning
signifying say what

Ethiopian breakdown
underbelly tussle
lose the facts just keep the hustle
leave your fine-tooth comb at home

if your complexion is a mess
our elixir spells skin success
you'll have appeal bewitch be adored
hechizando con crema dermoblanqueadora

what we sell is enlightenment
nothing less than beauty itself
since when can be seen in the dark
what shines hidden in dirt

double dutch darky
take kisses back to Africa
they dipped you in a vat
at the wacky chocolate factory

color we've got in spades
melanin gives perpetual shade
though rhythm's no answer to cancer
pancakes pale and butter can get rancid

the essence lady
wears her irregular uniform
a pinstripe kente
syncopation suit

she dreads her hair
sprung from lock down
under steel teeth press gang
galleys upstart crow's nest

eyes lashed half open
look of lust bitten
lips licked the dusky
wicked tongued huzzy

am I your type
that latest lurid blurb
was all she wrote her
highbrow pencil broke

self-made woman gets
the hang -- it's a stretch
she's overextended weaving
many spindly strands on her hair loom

walking through the alley
all night alone
stalked by a shadow
throw the black cat a bone

step off bottom woman
when the joint gets jinky
come blazing the moment
the hens get hincty

raw souls get ready
people rock steady
the brown gals in this town
know how to roll the woodpile down

dry bones in the valley
turn over with wonder
was it to die for our piece
of buy 'n' buy pie chart

hot water cornbread
fresh water trout
God's plenty the preacher shouts
while the congregation's eating out

women of honey harmonies offer
alfalfa wild flower buckwheat and clover
to feed Oshun who has sweet teeth
and is pleased to accept their gift

these mounts that heaven touched
saints sleep in their beds
distress is hushed by dream when
they allow the bird to lift their heads

ain't your fancy
handsome gal
feets too big
my hair don't twirl

from hunger call
on the telephone
asking my oven for
some warm jellyroll

if I can't have love
I'll take sunshine
if I'm too plain for champagne
I'll go float on red wine

what you can do
is what women do
I know you know
what I mean, don't you

arrives early for the date
to tell him she's late
he watches her bio clock balk on seepy time
petals out of rhythm docked for trick crimes

flunked the pregnancy test
mistimed space probe, she aborted
legally blind justice, she miscarried
scorched and salted earth, she's barren

when Aunt Haggie's chirren throws
an all originals ball
the souls ain't got a stray word
for the woman who's wayward

dead to the world
let earth receive her piece
let every dark room repair her heart
let nature and heaven give her release

39

moon, whoever knew you
had a high IQ until tonight
so high and mighty bright
poets salute you with haiku

fixing her lips to sing
hip strutters ditty bop
hand-me-down dance of ample
style stance and substance

black-eyed pearl
around the world girl
somebody's anybody's
yo-yo fulani

occult iconic crow
solo mysterioso
flying way out
on the other side of far

the royal yellow sovereign
a fragile grass stained widow
black veins hammered gold
folded hands applaud above a budding

flat back green and easy
stacked for salt meat seasoning
some fat on that rack
might make her more tasty

a frayed one way slave's
sassy fast sashay
fastens her smashing essay
sad to say yes unless

your only tongue turns
me loose excuse my French
native speaker's opening act
a tight clench in the dark theater

software design for
legible bachelors
up to their eyeballs
in hype-writer fonts

didn't call
you ugly -- said
you was ruined
that's all

pass the paperbag
whether vein tests
the wild blue
blood to the bone

spin the mix fast forward
mutant taint of blood
mongrel cyborg
mute and dubbed

poor stick doll
crucifix stiff
bent bird shutters
torn parasol

mellow elbow lengthy
fading cream and peaches
bleach burn lovingly
because she's worth it

ass is grassy ass is
ashy just like we do
such subtle cuts
clutter the difficult

trick rider circuitry
wash your mariney
lick and a promissory
end of story morning-glory

dressed as a priestess
she who carries water
mirrors mojo breasts
Yemoja's daughter

some loose orisha gathering
where blue meets blue
walk out to that horizon
tie her sash around you

how many heads of cowries
openmouthed oracles
drinking her bathwater
quench a craving for knowledge

kumbla of red feathers
tongues chant song
may she carry it well
and put it all down

tom-tom can't catch
a green cabin
ginger hebben as
ancestor dances in Ashanti

history written with whitening
darkened reels and jigs
perform a mix of wiggle
slouch fright and essence of enigma

a tanned Miss Ann startles
as the slaver screen's
queen of denial a bottle
brown as toast Egyptian

today's dread would awe
Topsy undead her missionary
exposition in what Liberia
could she find freedom to study her story

up from slobbery
hip hyperbole
the soles of black feet
beat down back streets

a Yankee porkchop
for your knife and fork
your fill of freedom
in Philmeyork

never trouble rupture
urban space fluctuates
gentrify the infrastructure
feel up vacant spades

no moors steady whores
studs warn no mares
blurred rubble slew of vowels
stutter war no more

get off your rusty dusty
give the booty a rest
you must be more than just musty
unless you're abundantly blessed

I can't dance don't chance it
if anyone asks I wasn't present
see I wear old wrinkles
so please don't press me

my head ain't fried
just fresh rough dried
ain't got to cook
nor iron it neither

you've seen the museum of famous hats
where hot comb was an artifact
now it's known that we use mum or numb our stresses
sometimes forget to fret about our tresses

heard about that gal
in Kansas City got meatballs
yes you shall have cake and eat
your poundcake on the wall

quickie brick houses
don't roll rickrack stones
or bats eyelashes rocks you
till bric-a-brac's got no home

ain't had chick to chirp nor child to talk
not pot to piss in, no dram to drink
get my hands on money marbles and chalk
I'll squeeze till eagle grin, till pyramid wink

tussy-mussy mufti
hefty duty rufty-tufty
flub dub terra incog
mulched hearts agog

hooked on phonemes imbued with exuberance
our spokeswoman listened for lines
heard tokens of quotidian
corralled in ludic routines

slumming umbra alums
lost some of their parts
getting a start
in the department of far art

monkey's significant uncle
blond as a bat
took off beat path
through tensile jungle

dark work and hard
though any mule can
knock down the barn
what we do best requires finesse

frizzly head
gumbo clay
skull drudgery
mojo handyman

crow quill and India
put th' ink in think
black cat in the family tree
hairy man's Greek to me

krazy kongograms
recite the fatal bet
missiles of affection
dingbat flings brick velvet

bean pole
lightning rod
bottle tree
tall drink

go on sister sing your song
lady redbone señora rubia
took all day long
shampooing her nubia

she gets to the getting place
without or with him
must I holler when
you're giving me rhythm

members don't get weary
add some practice to your theory
she wants to know is it a men thing
or a him thing

wishing him luck
she gave him lemons to suck
told him please dear
improve your embouchure

tomboy girl with cowboy boots
takes coy bow in prom gown
your orange California suits
you riding into sundown

lifeguard at apartheid park
rough, dirty, a little bit hard
broken blossom poke a possum
park your quark in a hard aardvark

a wave goodbye a girl
bred on the Queen Mary
big legged gal
how come you so contrary

let the birds pick her
make a nest of her hair
let the rootman conjure
her to stare and stir air

sauce squandering sassy cook
took a gander bumped a pinch of goose
skinned squadroon cotillion filled
uptown ballroom with squalid quadrille

don't eat no crow, don't you know
ain't studying about taking low
if I do not care for chitterlings
'tain't nobody's pidgin

Hawkins was talking
while I kept on walking
now I'm standing in my tracks
stepping back on my abstract

if not a don't at least a before
skin of a rubber chicken
these days I ignore
I'm less interested in

gaudy colors you flaunt
how loud you sirens behave
the man drowns in your salt
you revive him with a wave

restless born-agains
outlaw beat machines
yet the drums roll on
let the churchy femmes say amen

downhome quotes
the human figure
carries the vote
over dead signatures

tasty brown sugar molasses
accused of wide abandoned laughter
nothing left to lose or gain
delicate powder melts in the brain

ass can't cash
mere language
sings scat logic
talking shit up blues creek

no miss thing
ain't exactly rude
just exercising
her right to bare attitude

rope rash lads
rubber whiplashed
breakneck beauty
can be had

money's mammy mentions
some chit chat
getting paid
to take it like that

singed native skin
binging island sun
shines on shingles
shunning unhinged singles

ghetto-bound pretos
call on dark petro
powers that be fighting
when there's no money to lighten

historic old haunts where
creole servants get the door
or sweep up dusty graveyards
with zombi esprit decor

tropical fantasy
punany as you want to be
coked bottled bodies
with fantacide faces

mutter patter simper blubber
murmur prattle smatter blather
mumble chatter whisper bubble
mumbo-jumbo palaver gibber blunder

colored hearing colored
sounds darker
back vowels lower
down there deeper

churn and dasher
mortar and pestle
bumped your head
on a piece of cornbread

I didn't went to go
swing slow zydeco
so those green chariots
light your eyes up

massa had a yeller
macaroon a fetter
in his claptrap
of couth that shrub rat

sole driver rode
work hard on demand
he's the man
just as long as he can

outside MOMA
on the sidewalk
Brancusi's blonde
sells ersatz Benin bronzes

Joe Moore never
worked for me -- oh moaner
you shall be free
by degrees and pedigrees

handheld interview cuts to
steady voice over view
extra vagrants gobble up the scenery
this camera's gonna roll all over you

discarded barnacled bard
grinning with bad dentures
remembering coonskin adventures
in your hackneyed backyard

solar flares scrambled
bell bottoms sunnyside
signal didn't she ramble
those black holes backslide

drippy tresses bagged
in plastic do-rag
sensible heel in execu-drag
whose dress sucks excess

O rose so drowsy in
my flower bed your pink
pajamas ziz-zag into
fluent dreams of living ink

carve out your niche
reconfigure the hybrid
back in the kitchen
live alone, buy bread

your backbone slip
sliding silk hipped
to the discography
of archival sarcophagi

pregnant pause conceived
by doorknob insinuation
and onset animal
laminates no DNA

manx cat rations
pussy got your tongue
angoraphobic x-man
sex kitten operation

blow hair died
a natural death
laid aside glory fried
flashing a panacea

her realness
was wild at the time
leastwise they tell me
it was legendary

chez lounge lizard
hip-hop hazard
master beats and breaks
baby's back-up aches

a strict sect's
hystereotypist hypercorrects
the next vexed hex
erects its noppy text

where whirly Saturn
turns worldly girls
wear curly perms
affirm natty pattern

chenille feely zeroes
fuzzy nooky fumble
your nu-nile omieros
our frondy jungle

lucky lucre dream dujour
a lotto numbing ventured dues
paid off a doler
and another don't

rap attacks your tick
cold fusion's licks
could make you sick
nobody's dying in this music

womanish girl meets mannish boy
whose best buddy's a doggish puppy
he dictate so dicty, she sedate so seditty
the girl get biggity when the boy go uppity

I'm down to Saint James Infirmary
getting tested for HIV
the needle broke, the doctor choked
and told me I'd croak from TB

did I say nobody's dying
well I lied, like last night
I was lying with your mama who was crying
for all the babies born in Alabama

marry at a hotel, annul 'em
nary hep male rose sullen
let alley roam, yell melon
dull normal fellow hammers omelette

divine sunrises
Osiris's irises
his splendid mistress
is his sis Isis

creole cocoa loca
crayon gumbo boca
crayfish crayola
jumbo mocha-cola

warp maid fresh
fetish coquettish
a voyeur leers
at X-rated reels

spaginzy spagades
splibby splabibs
choice voice noise
gets dress and breath

slave-made artifact
your salt-glazed poetry
mammy manufacture
jig-rig nitty-gritty

fast dance synched up so
coal burning tongues
united surviving ruin
last chance apocalypso

broke body stammering spirit
been worked so hard
if I heard a dream
I couldn't tell it

pipsqueak at sea
snail shell matrices
whirlwind gig
minkisi indigo

rose is off the bloomers
storm in the womb
an old broom scatters
shotgun rumor

hip chicks ad glib
flip the script
spinning distichs
tighter than Dick's hatband

buttermilk haystack
woodpile inkwell
darktown brierpatch
buckwheat bottom sugarhill

mulatos en el mole
me gusta mi posole
hijita del pueblo moreno
ya baila la conquista

chant frantic demands
in the language
bring generic offerings to
a virgin of origins

yes I've tried in vain
never no more to call your name
and in spite of all reminders
misremembered who I am

ghosts brush past
surprise arrival at
these states of flux
that flow and flabbergast

cross color ochre with stalk of okra
that prickly lover told her
she tastes like an Okie
yet lacks the rich aroma of a smoker

those cloudy days I'd fly
from the icy airport
while you tried to breathe life
into your bucktoothed scarecrow

if you turned down the media
so I could write a book
then you could look me up
in your voluminous recyclopedia

raped notes torn
as deep ones parted
the frank odor of the rodeo
the reason a person

pretend you don't understand
reckless letters I wrote
can't read my crooked hand
decode those cryptic notes

you were longing to belong
thoughts wander where have you gone
Zuli made her bed at home
that's why we don't get along

her red flag is flying
with bright sequins shining
her heart of swords
is its own reward

feed the spirits or they'll
chew on your soul
you'll be swallowed and digested
by a riled-up crocodile

married the bear's daughter
and ain't got a quarter
now you're playing the dozens
with your uncle's cousins

sitting here marooned
in limbo quilombo
ace coon ballooned up
without a parachute

use your noodle for
more than a hatrack
act like you got the sense
God gave a gopher

couldn't fold the tablecloth
can't count my biscuits
think you're able to solve
a figure, go ahead and risk it

when memory is unforgiving
mute eloquence
of taciturn ghosts
wreaks havoc on the living

intimidates intimates
polishing naked cactus
down below a bitter buffer
inferno never froze over

to deaden the shock
of enthusiastic knowledge
a soft body when struck
pale light or moderate

smooth as if by rubbing
thick downward curving
bare skin imitative
military coat made of this

mister arty martyr
a jackass to water
changing partners in
the middle of a scream

bereft of flavor
for lack of endeavor
he chooses a heifer
and loses forever

delirious boozer
he smoothes her sutures
removes a moocher
from her future

a thing of shreds and patches
hideous scarecrow she
puts teeth in any nightmare
of the man who sleeps with matches

slashing both your wrists
to look tough and glamorous
dead shot up in the art gallery
you can keep your shirt on already

while I slip into something more funkable
rub-a-dub with rusty man abrasions
was I hungry sleepy horny or sad
on that particular occasion

invisible incubus took up
with a cunning succubus
a couple of mucky-mucks
trying to make a buck

slandered and absurdly slurred
wife divorced her has-been
last man on earth hauls ass to the ash can
his penis flightier than his word

precious cargo up crooked alleys
mules and drugs
blood on the lilies
of the fields

drive by lightning
let Mississippi rip
catch some sense
if you get my drift

watch out for the wrecking crew
they'll knock you into the dirt
your attic will be in your basement
and you'll know how it feels to be hurt

a planet struck by fragments
of a shattered comet
tell it after the break
save it for the next segment

tabloid depravity
dirty snowball
held together
with weak gravity

"fool weed, tumble your
head off -- that dern wind
can move you, but
it can't budge me"

he couldn't help himself
he couldn't help it
he couldn't stop himself
nobody stopped him

blessed are stunned cattle
spavined horses bent under their saddles
blessed is the goat as its throat is cut
and the trout when it's gutted

Jesus is my airplane
I shall feel no turbulence
though I fly in a squall
through the spleen of Satan

in a dream the book beckoned
opened for me to the page
where I read the words
that were to me a sign

houses of Heidelberg
outhouse cracked house
destroyed funhouse lost
and found house of dead dolls

two-headed dreamer
of second-sighted vision
through the veil
she heard her call

they say she alone smeared herself
wrote obscenities on her breast
snatched nappy patches from her scalp
threw her own self on a heap of refuse

knowing all I have is dearly bought
I'll take what I can get
pick from the ashes
brave the alarms

another video looping
the orange juice execution
her brains spilled milk
on the killing floor

if she entered freely
drank freely -- did that not mean
she also freely gave herself to one and all --
then when was she no longer free?

we believed her
old story she told
the men nodded at her face
dismissing her case

debit to your race
no better for you -- lost
gone off demented
throwing unevenhanded

disappeared undocumented workhorse
homeless underclass breeder
dissident pink collard criminal
terminal deviant indigent slut

riveted nailed to the table
crumpled muddied dream stapled
in her face mapped folded back
to the other side of the facts

that her body bleeds
is no surprise
a fragment bursts and color seeps
through her camouflage

bannered behind her
braid unfurled
extended she lean aiming
breaking the ribbon

kink konk crisp crinkle
my monkey's off his head
he wears my hat that
helps me think a little

zipped into high-tech overalls
suited to her lightfoot boots
kicking her heels up
and away beyonder

just as I am I come
knee bent and body bowed
this here's sorrow's home
my body's southern song

cram all you can
into jelly jam
preserve a feeling
keep it sweet

so beautiful it was
presumptuous to alter
the shape of my pleasure
in doing or making

proceed with abandon
finding yourself where you are
and who you're playing for
what stray companion

SINGING HORSE PRESS TITLES

Ammiel Alcalay, *the cairo notebooks*. 1993, $9.50.
Asa Benveniste, *Invisible Ink*. 1989, $4.00.
Charles Bernstein, *Artifice of Absorption*. 1987, $5.00.
Julia Blumenreich, *Meeting Tessie*. 1994, $6.00.
Rachel Blau DuPlessis, *Draft X: Letters*. 1990, $6.00.
Robert Fitterman, *Among the Cynics*. 1989, $4.00.
Karen Kelley, *Her Angel*. 1992, $4.00.
Kush, *The End Befallen Edgar Allen Poe–1849*. 1982, $2.00.
David Miller, *Unity*. 1981, $3.00.
Harryette Mullen, *Muse & Drudge*. 1995, $12.50.
Harryette Mullen, *S*PeRM**K*T*. 1992, $6.00.
Gil Ott, *Traffic (Books I & II)*. 1985, $2.50.
Ted Pearson, *Soundings*. 1980, OP.
Rosmarie Waldrop, *Differences for Four Hands*. 1984, OP.
Craig Watson, *Drawing A Blank*. 1980, OP.
Vassilis Zambaras, *Aural*. 1984, $2.00.